HUM DUM

A COLLECTION

Saniya Ruqiah Ahmed

Hum Dum | A Poetry Collection

© 2024 Strange Inc and Saniya Ruqiah Ahmed

Hardback: 979-8-9888848-3-5
Paperback: 979-8-9888848-4-2
E-Book 979-8-9888848-5-9
Cover Design by Hina Arshad
Edited by Laura El Alam

Published by Strange Inc, a nonprofit publishing house based in New York. Our mission is to elevate the authentic voices of Muslim women.
Email: hello@strangeincorporated.org
Website: www.strangeincorporated.org
Phone: +1 (347) 560-8334

Disclaimer: *The views and opinions shared in this anthology are those of the author. Strange Inc do not endorse any personal view of the authors on any platform. Strange Inc adhere to the widely accepted traditional, orthodox doctrine of Ahlus Sunnah.*

Word Of Praise For Hum Dum

I am very picky about poetry so I tend to be skeptical whenever I pick up a new collection. I always brace myself for forced rhymes and trite messages. My pessimism was unfounded, I am happy to say, with *Hum Dum*, which turned out to be a delight to read.

Saniya Ruqiah Ahmed is a gifted poet whose words – while clearly personal, specific, and heartfelt– reflect so many people's experiences. Children of immigrants, American Muslims, people with one foot in their family's culture and another foot in American society, those who love Islam and strive to please Allah, women who are ambitious and modern and simultaneously attached to their heritage and religion, Muslims who revere their parents and try to make them proud . . . all of these readers (and more) will find inspiration and relatability in Ahmed's poems.

I think it's a rare talent to be able to write poetry that is Islamic but not preachy, wholesome but not infantile, and respectful of tradition yet modern and realistic. Ahmed has achieved that amazing balance, MashaAllah, and I highly recommend this book.

— Laura El Alam, editor and author of Award-Winning Book,

Made From The Same Dough

Hum Dum is simultaneously a prayer and love letter to the rich overlap of Muslim devotion and Indian heritage. Assertively experimenting with the boundaries of form, while confidently preserving several languages and traditions, Saniya Ahmed's debut poetry book is a humble ode to her ancestry, and is sure to elicit content sighs and a resonant 'Ameen' from all readers alike.

— Sara Bawany, author of *Quarter Life Crisis* and *(w)holehearted*,

Lead Writing Mentor at House of Amal

Hum Dum is a poetry collection that inspires hope, pride, and tenderness. Saniya Ahmed weaves together themes of the diaspora, from generational resilience to the complexity of the 3rd culture kid, with a dash of romance and yearning. This book is a beautiful ode to family, heritage, and the spirit of justice and radical love.

— Amal Kassir, Spoken Word Poet, founder of House of Amal, and author of *Scud Missile Blues*

It is rare to encounter poetry that resonates so profoundly with both the soul and the mind. Saniya's words in this captivating collection will grip you from the very first line. Her artistry shines as she gives voice to the unspoken language of the heart. I found it impossible to put this book down—reading it in one sitting, only to be left yearning for more. Truly, a stunning and evocative masterpiece.

— Kashmir Maryam, Founding Director of *Heal Therapy Clinic*

Saniya's book Hum Dum is a powerful and introspective reflection on identity, strength and love, gorgeously platformed through a tented hand in poetry. It is a beautiful reminder of our own relationship to culture, religion and all that which makes us human. A highly recommended read for those who want depth and authenticity in their life.

— Aishah Alam, Founder of Strange Inc. publishing, Certified Integrative Somatic Practitioner, and author of *The Woke Writer*

About Hum Dum

Hum Dum in Urdu at its simplest can be translated as companion, but its true essence goes much deeper: derived from Farsi, 'Ham' (ﮨﻢ) means 'we' or 'us,' and 'Dam' (ﺩﻡ) means 'breath.' When combined, 'Ham Dam' literally translates to the one you breathe with. These pieces strive to do and be the same. The intention of the poetry collection is to capture companionship, family, home, and love. A breath of fresh air to the themes of identity of a first-generation Muslim Indian American woman navigating the turmoil and revolution to exist in completion, this collection aims to provide reflection, to bring voice to words that begin as roars and fall as tears, to kindle wholeness for all our souls. This is a poetry collection to honor a legacy beyond just the author; may it bring you solace and ease.

HUM DUM

A COLLECTION

Contents

INTRODUCTION

Hum Dum[1]

The intention is

To capture

companionship, family, home, and love.

To breathe

with my pen, heartbeat in hand.

To find

warmth and solace in script.

To ease

the trials of longing.

To soothe

my open wounds.

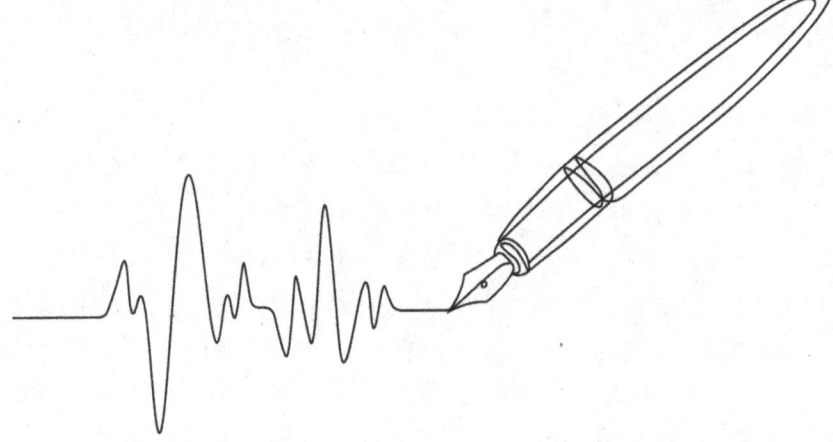

---

1   Hum dum in Urdu means companion. Derived from Farsi, it literally translates to "the one you breathe with."

Hum Dum: a collection

For love

    lost and found.

For ehsaas

    which stirs the heart.

For reflection

    that widens the mind.

For words

    that fall as tears.

For my soul

    and yours.

COMPANIONS:
of family

I live on the wings of prayers

That carry me to heights
unheard and unseen by those before me.
The hopes and dreams unreached
weigh heavy as I soar, but
the prayers ground me in a path
carved carefully by those I love.

I live on the prayers of my father's father
who reached the Gates before I was born.
It is his endless pleas for success in this life
and the next that were echoed as inheritance.
And so I stand here today,
on the prayers
of a voice I've never heard.

I live on the prayers of my mother's father
who taught me everything I know about this deen.
It is in his shade that I strive to live a life
worthy of being an Ummati.
And so I stand here today,
on the familiar prayers of
his shining star, praying we reunite in the galaxies beyond.

I live on the prayers of my father's mother
who slept with our photos tucked under her pillow,
her grandchildren thousands of miles away, whom she loved deeply without divide.
It is because of her desire for cultured children
I stay rooted today
on the fulfilled prayers
that she'll witness when we meet again.

I live on the prayers of my mother's mother
who laughs at religiosity, but prays for my future religiously.
It is her supplication for my success tied tightly in sadaqah
that keeps me upright today,
on the prayers
mirroring promised fulfillment in her hopeful eyes.

I live on the wings of prayers
supplicated by my elders.
Those here and those there.
The prayers that reach beyond me,
yet surround me in
every step I take in this life, and
every step towards the Heavens.

My descendants will soar on the wings of my prayers.
Forethought by my ancestors
lifted by the winds of my tongue and
echoed into the ears of the inheritors
like the azan that begins the end.
Until we meet in the land of endless flight,
may we carry each other up to the seven skies above

Ameen.

Visionaries

I am the child of poets
who explain the world
around us with songs of the cicadas

My mother taught me to find rhyme with rhythm
blossom within downpour peacealongsidewar
floods and the parting of the sea
so if you can only see the bad, it's time to
adjust to a more just lens

my father taught me to read between the lines
to hear the heartbeat of silence
painting portraits with white space
because sometimes we say what we mean
when we say nothing at all

my long lineage of visionaries
some unlettered some degreed
but all those with iman-heavy ilm,
persons who saw our purpose
in spreading salam and practicing the prophetic way
we must elevate the Words and
present our akhlaq shining from the noor of
iman and aqeedah

the Vision is of a people on the path of ihsan paved
from teacher to student
from school to scholar
from poet to listener
to seek understanding to be understood and
pillars of admiration for our Creator and His
creations sustain the passage of the Vision

blessed am I, the descendent of visionaries and ancestor to inheritors
grounded in the love of this Vision, stretching beyond the blanket of blue skies

Legacy of Laborers, Homemakers, and Everything in Between

If I lose my job now and die,
the roof over your head will vanish
my father says as he agrees to yet another year of
working under heat of no A.C. and angry stares.
The agony
slips through his lips
and shatters my young soul.
He lives sacrificing self-respect
and making himself smaller
just to guarantee we live larger than life.

When they lower me into my grave, you will call out to say
'Wait, I need my mother to do one more thing before she goes'
my mother says as she stirs tonight's fresh salan,
and calculates the profit of others while losing her own.
The exhaustion
falls from her tongue
and lands on the threads of my budding ehsaas.
She lives working to death and then
standing some more to uphold the home
just to make our lives easier than hers.

My parents
who labored their entire lives for their children
seem to think they didn't do
anything monumental
but
built an empire
of knowledge, access, and pathways
with their honest, hard work.

What an incredibly heavy legacy
to leave for us
to carry on.

To my future family,

I don't know about your current reality // but let me tell you something I do know // morality and mortality // we don't have long on this earth // so make the most of what you got // don't let your dreams rot // don't just live and let live // give but don't take // it takes one mistake to make or break someone else // so think about what you're doing // the path that you're taking // and see if anyone gets hurt or helped in the making.

To my future husband,
I'll be honest // you're a lucky man // I'm powerful and you're my match // so we'll attach // our minds // our dreams // our lives // and be united and strong // for the record // I'm never wrong // we'll stand shoulder to shoulder // hand in hand // fists raised high // look at how far we've come // we've been battling hatred and discrimination // in this nation // to make our world a better place // and erase the dirt off a concept called "loving thy neighbor" // by loving each other and everyone around us // may Allah keep our marriage happy and healthy // Ameen // I mean // I know we'll have our rainy days but that's what rain boots are for // and you can bet I'm gonna make us dance in the rain // there's no point in waiting for the sun because // I'm already here // but you can be the moon and // we'll balance each other out // but our children // oh they'll be our stars // let us pass onto them what has been passed down to us // and trust our cultured upbringings // and the strengths of our deen.

To my future children,
My darling daughters and my sweet sons // this world is a dark, dark place // but your innocent faces shine bright // and eventually that innocence will turn into a fierce flame for justice // a torch against evils // a lamp to

guide you on your way // and I pray we teach you well // we will arm you with the ability to count and speak // so that you can calculate your own worth // so that no one can ever silence you // your defiance defines us // as a people // as a family // go do your homework and clean up your room // catch every corner and crevice // oppression is designed a mess // so we can't rest until all people are free // this isn't about you or me // it's about us all // your Baba and I will try and keep you safe and secure // but there's no magic cure to the -isms and -phobias // that doesn't mean we can't teach you to carry passion in your hearts // and do your parts // your future is not bleak // even though it reeks // of past havoc and mayhem // it's up to you to make it past.

And to my baby girls in particular,
Darlings if anyone ever asks y'all why you wear the hijab or why you don't // I want you to look them in the eye and know in your heart // that you answer to Allah and Allah alone // carry yourselves with strength and you're ready to roll // not everyone deserves an answer // and it's a bitter thing to learn sweet souls // but Allah loves you // and so do Mumma and Baba // so if you ever choose to stand up // fires will erupt // dams will break // grounds will shake with the power of your iman.

To my future family,
With hard work and play // I've paved my way // to you and I hope our souls // have fused and forever intertwine // our paths never a straight line // but one we'll walk together regardless // with strength // with courage // with hope

With love, your Saniya
Forever.

Father's Unspoken Love

My father's eyes dampen and
I wonder what it is sometimes.

What is it about that scene in that one movie
or about this country song on the radio
and that dialogue on cable TV?

How can a man so strong,
so stoic and serious,
be moved to tears at the mention
of love for family, Allah, and His Rasul ﷺ?

My father who speaks only with loudness,
many times with anger and frustration,
with rough edges chiseling
discipline with care.

My father who puts adventure before work
and laughs joyously like a sky that rumbles,
with a firm determination to give his children everything
their hearts desire, and his.

My father who always made time for
days full of trampolining, swimming, and bike riding,
teaching us the *right* way to hold the flashlight while he fixed
whatever needed mending.
My father who works hard,
with toughened callouses to prove
how well he always provided
for his family.

My father whom many don't understand
or care to understand because of his
firm stances on international politics
and far-sighted vision for the Ummah.

Lately, I see him wiping his eyes
and I am unsure whether his remembrance is of us,
my grandparents, or of Divinity.
But now my heart tightens too

at that scene in that one movie
with this country song on the radio
and that dialogue on cable TV.

Now, my soul sees through my father's eyes,
and I can hear his unspoken love.

Ammi the Jannati

Motherhood begins from the rooted depths of the womb / and leads to the gardens of Jannah / it is more than birthing babies and keeping children alive / the provider provides / the nurturer nurtures / each parent gets their share of divine responsibilities / somehow it seems like Ammis have the lion's share / while maintaining the work ethic of lionesses / the small supplemental moments underappreciated / while she maintains balance between / healing herself and / fulfilling her motherhood / But still / still she / provides / still she / nurtures / it's her raising hands to the Lord / when we have our heads bowed in our books / it's her bowls of fruit and fresh chai / as our stress cycles night into day.

Ammi isn't my friend / she said we can't be / not because she didn't want the bond / but because she was so much more than that / the walls of her womb were my first home / her chest my rizq / her lap my head's cradle / her prayer palms and arms carry me to this day / her heart fragments in sixths / a piece for each child / yet she reminds me of mine every day / no one more / no one less / but we all yearn for imbalance / in our favor.

it's simple nature of the mother / one who gives and gives / who we revere / (sometimes) / but in this life / by us ungratefuls / Ammi never truly receives reciprocation of the same / love / dedication / or care / there's a reason that mothers are held / in high esteem across cultures / there's a reason that it is / your mother / your mother / your mother - and then your father / there is a reason / Jannah's Gates must be adorned by the calls of mothers / ones we all recognize as home / ones that are the likely reason for us to reach here / in the first place / the palaces for mothers must be in communion with the Mothers of us all / their jihads tirelessly unending.

If I could be a fraction of the kind of mother / Ammi is / then maybe my Lord will give me / a piece of paradise / beneath my feet / too.

COMPANIONS:
of community

Muslim Indian Diaspora

We are woven into the nation's mental textiles
    tailored to being the bad guys
in cinema and beyond
    we bear the brunt of fasads in every crevice of the country and
drown in poverty and lack of education
    we are removed from the national count
like we are unworthy of mention, of inclusion
    as if we are not tortured, harassed, discriminated against
by hundreds of thousands on a daily basis
    as if our mere existence is an inconvenience
but we carry the Indian essence with culinary prowess
    our masala mixed into this country's very foundation
our literary talents articulated the national identity
    while accused of being spies from across the border
we held equal involvement as freedom fighters
    yet suffer unequal treatment thereafter
we fought for collective liberation of all people
    but were targeted for elimination of our people
so when my friends of the Muslim diaspora
    proudly don their country's flag
I grapple with my tricolored stain
    uneasy at the thought of being
proud to be from my country
    my country where we are scapegoated
and politicians openly call for our genocide,
    and the world watches and stares and doesn't even blink

while extremism leads to death at the hands of these colonial games

and somehow we're the terrorists

no matter the country

so are you Muslim American or are you Indian American?

golden without a silver spoon

nawabi but only within four minars

building both watans and still being erased from the silhouette

both, I am both

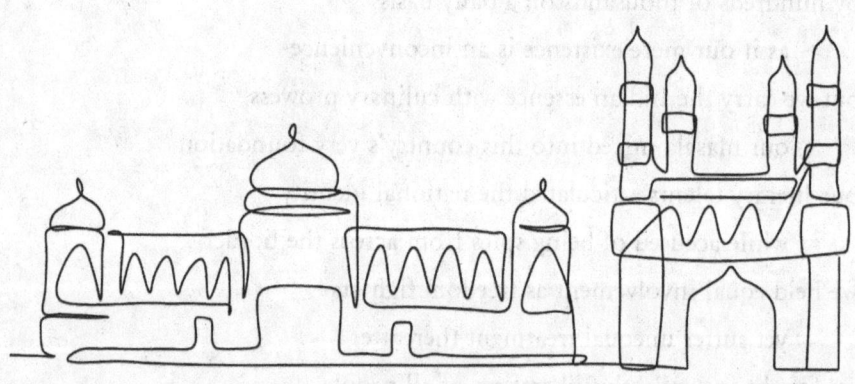

How do I explain to the immigrant generation

that they can't project their insecurities

    on me just because they couldn't maintain

        culture, language, or heritage in their families

        that

I am not one-dimensional "American"

    just because they never lived a life

        rooted in two different places at once

        that

being cloaked in this flag means I didn't

    experience the same oppressions but generational

        trauma is woven into the very fabric of my genetic code

        that

I carry faint battle scars of

    british rule and traces of

        soolis etched into my skin

        that

my veins transfuse blood into the body

    crossing partitions

        like old blood spilled before me at new borders

        that

the swords of conformity

    are still set at my throat

        from a culture that doesn't surround me

        that

my bones hardened with

    the demands of inqilab, the coded

        whispers of freedom and fiery fights for justice

        that

I am forged from a country
        that is foreign to me and I live
           in a country that labels me foreign
               that
I was birthed from my Motherland so
        no matter how far the umbilical has to stretch
           I am still bound to the land of my ancestors

First Gen. Success

My roots were uprooted
and I was planted here, in American soil
as a seed of hope for a better life
for accomplishments my parents couldn't even dream of.

Immigrant parents
they teach us spelling and long division
how to identify herds and hurdles
longitude and latitude
never letting us rest
giving us the recipe to success
the attitude for altitude
the absolute amplitude for making them proud.
The women and men who work away

entire days
deserve to watch their children
reach high enough
to pick stars out of the night sky.

But even if we try, we can never repay them
for the sacrifices they made so
instead, we will find a way to bring
gardens to their feet
peace to their minds
ease to their sore hands and
we will soar with them
because of them
to the highest peaks and give their hearts eternal joy.

And in the end, even if we feel like we aren't good enough,
we were given this chance in the Land of Opportunity
to open doors for generations to come and maybe
we'll find a little something for ourselves along the way.

Our Ancestors Did Not Breathe This Air: but I do, and so do you

after the collection <u>Our Ancestors Did Not Breathe This Air</u>

My heart aches for her mother to accept the finished "Carving"

    in the gardens of paradise

    where reunion awaits

    in the most beautiful of ways

And it aches for the "Morning Echoes" I heard when Nana Baba returned,

    where I pray for my own reunion with those I love.

    We love and we hope and we fear and we pray

    for home, reunion, and justice.

I've always been known for my intensity when "i ask for Justice"

    protesting in the streets, raising my fist in solidarity

    prostrating in sajdah, raising my palms to the Most Just

    progressing in systems, raising the hammer to tear down oppression.

But it's because I don't want to be erased and in "A Statement for the Confused"

    it's clear that I'm proud to be Indian Muslim

    even though the paradox confuses and frustrates me,

    my heritage is my truth, and nothing anyone says is gonna change that.

While I'm still "Alive," I pray the rain washes my soul of sins

    when I make wudu with storm clouds,

    when the recitations of my ancestors

    settle on my tongue and echo in my ears.

When it's my turn to reach "the final destination,"

    I hope I'm not forgotten and

    I hope these Jannati poets remember me for the prayers I make

    for the peace they gave me with their pieces

And I hope the prayers of my ancestors and elders, of my Dada, "Dadi", Nana, Nanni

    are enough for me to meet them in the eternal resting place

    and I hope my prayers for all of them are

    worth something on their scales.

My tears fall "in remembrance of the One"

    at my own prayers at the masjid, my pleas for wholeness

    at my own tears that fell on Khatm-e-Qur'an, pleading for an Answer

    at my own marvel of community that I prayed for, that prayed for me.

My taste buds tingle on my tongue thinking of "My Lunch Box: The Exotic Bazaar"

    of my mummy's treasures coated in silver and in gold

    and I wonder how I'll pack my descendants' tiffins with such vibrance

    of a home and of roots they've branched even farther from.

But for now, I end the collection wondering if I will ever be "Enough"

    to be spoken about by my ancestors in Jannah,

    to save my people, our humanity, the world

    with my paper and pen or with my policy and medicines.

And for these women who paved the way before me in verse and beyond, I "Search"

    for my tomorrow and I realize an ode is in order:

    they are enough. And because they are,

    InshaAllah, one day I will be too.

All the words I love are poems

after Michelle Peñaloza

aaghaaz	the light that peaks across the horizon to welcome the day
afroz	illuminates grass blades dancing with dew, like
gulshan	bloomed jasmine braided into midwest winds, steady even in
tufaan	waves crashing like dialects do, storms stirring the soul with
talab	heavy aches, gnawing hunger, agonizing thirst, desperate for a
rahnumaa	guide who can shower me with rains of knowledge, of joy like
rhim jhim	light drizzles that mimic silver anklets twinkling in laughter; your
ruhaniyat	soulfulness hears the whispers of when oceans meet the sky, with
tajasus	curiosity you find in intricate twists of street-side jalebi, we bring
tabdeeli	revolution with butterfly wings together & I will cross any, every
dehleez	threshold that tries to contain me in one tongue because a single
chingari	spark is but the start of a soul-blazed wildfire

Darkness Within

The darkness beckons me with instability and uncertainty
unable to see with clarity, I am surrounded by a deafening silence
one that defines me as lonely and defeated,
who succumbed to her sins and licked her wounds just to
find herself barely alive in the first place
the waves crash against a moonless sky
where despairs drown me at nightfall
the test of times I've failed are nothing but a deep dive
into nothingness, where I am and will be nothing
but a woman who carries callouses from generations before
of what a woman can be, of struggle, of dampened hopes and dreams
in darkness, there is no hope and bountiful misery;
with company of the shaiyateen
the soul is lost and unguided and
without the feeling of God
I am trapped in a grave without illumination

Warrior Woman

I carry the burdens and battle scars of / a warrior woman / women endure and struggle to survive / we carry generations and / build fortresses from our wombs and / shape nations of people from our kin / we cook and clean and / sweep away our own desires and dreams as we manage households / we take each stage of life / as a place to conquer / to complete and fulfill / we strategize our lightest personal losses / and maximize community gains / we are our own first / and last / lines of defense / from mother to daughter / we fold and recruit each other up the ranks / knowing we need more seats at the table / knowing we are needed to preserve the fate of our people / falsehood encircles us but / how can we be expected to mold like plastic / when we were welded into perfection / hardened by hardships / sharpened by inequities / we will fight / breaking glass ceilings / from the deepest trenches / boldly facing the fate / of relentless war

COMPANIONS:
of love

Paradise Lost

Today I've lost.

My paradise on earth:
the edge of my grandparents' bed
on Jummah afternoons
sipping chai, speaking of the spiritual
about the Gardens from which
we can never fall from grace.

I stare at empty chairs and filled spaces,
passing cars and strangers' eyes,
looking for home in storms that
douse me in remembrance.
We believe souls will meet again.
but somewhere deep in my being I know

in the next life,
I may not be worthy
of being in the presence of such incredible souls.
My Beloved ﷺ promised that
we will be with
Those we love.
And even if my love for Him and His Rasul ﷺ
isn't enough,
my grandfather's is
and he will be with
Those he loves.
inshaAllah.

And that's enough of Paradise for me.

Fruits of Labor

Immigrant parents'
love
is difficult to understand.
    Sometimes.
Our parents' love is
in season always,
within reach to pick and ever-present.
    Sometimes
not ripe with feeling
but plump with laborious efforts
and endless ehsaas.
    Sometimes
I made all your favorite dishes
after a long day at work
I'll get it for you right now
even though it's last minute and midnight
Make sure to eat if you're staying up late
since their bodies are tired but their hearts are still with you
    Always.
Refreshing is the nectar
of sweet truths
and shared growth in understanding.
    At the core, *I love you* isn't enough anyway.
Our parents scattered seeds that blossom as
orchards of love throughout our lives
and we reaped the harvest every step of the way.

The Things That Matter

In the case of culture v. potential spouse,
the matter is
where his forefathers are from
what his parents and siblings do
his degree
how much he earns.

The opposition is obsessed with trivial things
like whether the dialect they speak is
up to their standard
like whether his God-crafted features are
up to their standard
as if we set the measure of every golden ratio in existence.

If the opposed continues,
the evidence overwhelmingly points to
a clear indictment of imprisonment
confined in a marriage defined by cultural standards.
Terrifying are the odds of a life-long sentence
if the opposition is favored for someone that supposedly matters.

The measures that matter are invaluable, like
if kindness drips from his lips when he speaks
if humbleness and confidence exude from his eyes
how gentle and honey-sweet his voice is, his words are and
if his love for me shines from his soul
and reflects in every fiber of his being.

In the case of culture v potential spouse,

the matter is

the measures that are valued are not the invaluable

so to pursue someone beyond the confines feels almost criminal.

I wonder what happens to the partners in life who commit the crime

of being someone who doesn't matter.

Full Flight

When winter trees are
bare and nests are
exposed, I wonder of the safety of the twigs that build a
home. Flying in rigid formation, migrating on the winds'
whim is not meant for
families or homes. But still
I dream of scouring the earth serving any and every
place I can, settling and unsettling over again. Relentlessly
I search, caressing my wings
with reassurance, convincing
myself with gentle stubbornness of the flights I wish to take.
As my life cycles, I pray the wind stays beneath my wings
even if the destinations shift.
I pray the nest fills, even as
I soar. To nest is to piece together our lives, one layer
at a time. The first strengthening the next, the way the
seasons fold into each other,
bringing familiarity and
a sense of home.

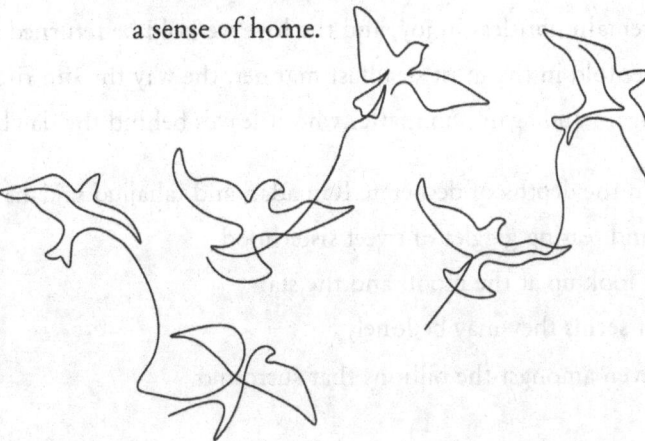

Star-Crossed Love

As I sit in this coffee shop typing away,
my eyes rest on two young lovers. They sit
facing each other, table aside,
their legs entangled and their hands resting in each others'
their soft whispers and quiet laughter.

Such enchantment of love: the man
who sees stars in her eyes. The one
who promises she'll be the center of his universe,
with the sun and moon balancing in one palm
while the stars and planets rest in the other.

The aunties orbit as my friends and I age, gushing
about our beauty and schooling, seemingly oblivious
to the realities of the marriage pursuit and dimmed success.
That ache for the fate of finding a kindred soul grows and
can only be soothed by supplication.

May the galaxy be at our spouses' fingertips, may
space and time favor their ambitions. May seven skies
remain limitless in joy, and the love we hold be returned to us
tenfold in the most steadfast manner, the way the sun rises
again and again, no matter who it leaves behind the day before.

In the depths of desperate Ramadan and tahajjud sajdahs
and teasing giggles of sweet sisterhood,
I look up at the moon and the stars
it seems they may be lonely
even amongst the billions that surround.

And it reminds me that if stars can cross,
then they can uncross;
those days of ethereal love are over
instead, I ask for a hand that doesn't let go
and a community that grows.

When the souls meet

if it's naseeb, of course
it's effortless like ujala of the rays

                                        peeking through leaves
                        and surrounds you like homecoming
the wind whispers sweet nothings
into your ear every morning

                        and reminds you that God created us in pairs
                        with new beginnings and reunions of the soul
the rain feels softer on your skin
the dua'as heavier

                                        you are the sunshine and
                                                he is the moonlight
together you make harmony
and inqilab rests on your lips

                                        because in this house,
                                        you want a revolutionary love
one that is fiercely rooted in Islam
and rebels against unforgiving cultural norms

                                                and overturns
                                        any ounce of self-oppression
home is an act of resistance
love is change making fisabillilah

                                        shackles of past pain fall
                        years of rusted armor come off
eyes meet with quiet embraces
cheeks rosy with hopes blooming of a new

horizon written in the stars eons ago

the breeze cooling whispered worries

God's gift wrapped in akhlaq

shading you with kindness and gentleness

living in answered dua'as

your soul now exists beyond yourself

so when the souls meet

it's naseeb of course

Rivers to the burning heart

By night   I have no one on this earth   but God.   And how ironic is that?
The Resident of the Throne in the Heavens   isn't even on earth, but
is still   Everywhere.   In daylight   there is routine and
responsibility   loneliness   in the crowds of tasks and to-do lists. It is
like   being filled to the brim of occupancy   mental or otherwise   but
ending up with   no one   and nothing   when the time comes.
          In noon skies   heartbreak pierces   with a high strung bow
the target   never failing to wound. It is   love crashing into me in waves
        like a beautiful spring sunrise   has tears rolling down my cheeks
          crisp autumn air makes a deep breath freeze in my chest
unsure of where to go   unsure of how to let go.   The night is void of it
all   and filled instead with longing
suffocation   and fear of seeing dreams that won't come true.   All I can
      hear is my own heartbeat   banging against my eardrums when I lay on
my pillow hoping that sleep will find me   before my thoughts do. It is
difficult to   breathe in darkness unsure   if relief will come   if hearts will
join   if troubles will ease.   These notions of company   do not dwell
well in my   mind and heart. Far too long have I waited   to feel
fulfilled   when I was simply looking for the wrong essence   of feeling
full.   To love deeply is   to hold space in every fiber of your being
                              space
to rejoice   to live   to understand   alongside someone
else. Grief is but love   that no longer has an earthly avenue   instead, our
whispering lips   graze the ground   to reach the seven skies above.
Our love   finding home in the sanctified Everlasting. For now it is easier to
cry myself to sleep.   Maybe the rivers will cool my burning heart
By morning.

COMPANIONS:
of faith

Remembrance

We have people in our lives
who are no longer here
but leave pieces of themselves in us.

Being their extension on earth
in company they didn't keep
helps revive them and

when Allah took away
the people we loved and cherished most
He gave us Himself and

what a beautiful elevation of their status:
we now remember our loved ones with Allah,
the All-Knowing and All-Seeing.

We carry
their character
in our conversations with Allah.

He replaces their absence
with His Presence
and our qadar of that.

We pray
we become righteous enough
for reunion.

Droplets of Mercy

Sins

wash away with

droplets that leave my body in

a serene, pure state of wudu, tears

wash away the ache in my soul, remembering

a God so Merciful that He weighs hundreds of my heavy

sins against mere particles of water. Atoms that collide and

fuse to create the substance we know. Each atom bears witness

to my sins, and to my Lord's erasure of them. From the skin of my

hands to the tips of my toes, my entire body cleansed in preparation

the way the rains ready soils for sowing. The rains drench my whole

person as I pray in solitude, in congregation. Renewal I pray is

coming. Quenching, softening, and soothing the burning in

in my heart that yearns for the rivers of

Jannatul Firdaus.

The Master and His Slave

In the Kingdom,
the King of Kings has His Throne on the seven skies,
ruling over this earth I walk on,
and every atom of the universe I can only imagine.
Rabbil Aalameen is my Master
and I am nothing but His humble slave, a servant
of His Majesty.
so why is it that when I obey my King,
I feel like royalty in my veil and my crown?
like a servant whose stature is elevated solely because she obeys
with love and ilm and aqeedah.

I strive to do what pleases my King,
and repent for what displeases.
I'm cloaked in the control of Al Wakeel,
the Best Disposer of Affairs,
and the uncertainty and anxiety fall from my person
like how not an autumn leaf falls
but that He knows of it.
I choose to be the slave of the Most Just and the Most Merciful
with aspirations to meet Him wrapped in His mercy
standing with unrelenting hope for
a piece of Paradise.

Majestic Muqarnas of the Masjid

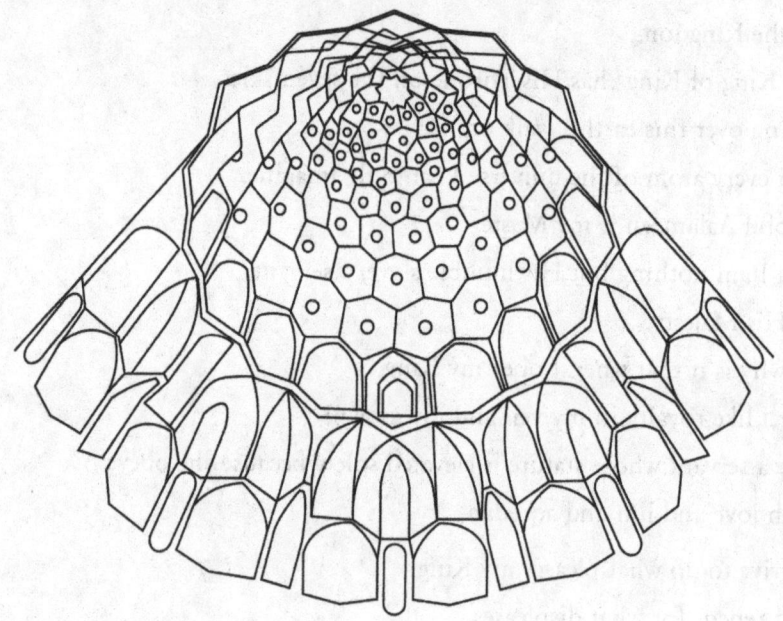

The muqarnas of masjid ceilings
reflect the magnificence and beauty
of the universe. With
honeycombs and semi-domes,
Islamic architects captured creation and, in some ways,
reflecting a piece of the Creator.
Mesmerizing are the corners decorated to adorn the direction of prayer,
and colorful tiles with mirrors and fantastical shapes
bring together the earth and the Heavens, the way the ocean kisses the sky
to capture a horizon. With
smooth seamless transitions from flat and vertical to
curved and horizontal, we are reminded of the mountains that pin down plains
and valleys that embrace the clouds. If

luminescence is the proposed ideal, maybe our path will become clear by
way of
The Illuminating One, and perhaps the smaller units of muqarnas
were kept whole solely by the will of the Almighty.
So when we sit in the masjid
and stare at the ceiling while speaking with Allah,
we are reminded of His Majesty, of His Greatness, of His Beauty.
Ya Muqtadir, the muqarnas beckon
us towards You. Perhaps this is why You called
on creation to create these crevices reminiscent of Your Divinity.

Gardener

I toil and turn
the soil of my soul,
hoping it becomes fertile
once more.

I want to sow seeds of sabr, shukr, and ihsan
so I can reap my Lord's mercy, forgiveness
and His eternal gardens
because I bear witness.

My heart yearns to grow,
but the cover of rust must fade first.
I must let go of my anger, heartbreak, impatience
and close the depth of wounds I nursed.

Iman and aqeedah
are the nutrients I need to feed
my heart to become stronger and steadfast
with prayers that my actions follow their lead.

The rains are coming.
I await anxiously with teardrops of my own
to soften the soil of my barren soul
and rake through rough patches, remove unturned stones.

I await the news of the moon sighting
and prepare for my own phases of transformation
in hopes that the moon tidings pull me
closer to my Lord's affirmation.

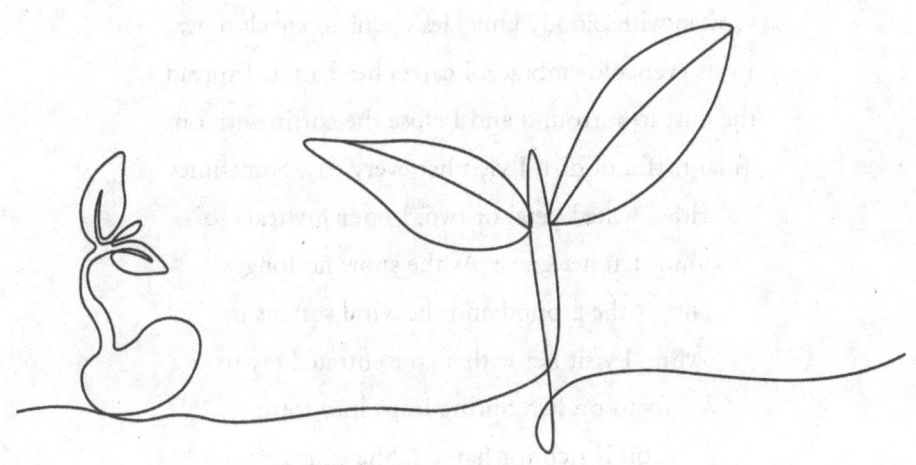

Buried for Renewal

In the bleak winter glare
I carry her through dying pine
and through frozen lands. I move aside
the barren dirt to bury her. Cracked soil I
soften with bloody knuckles opens to envelop her
in its ever-cold embrace. I caress her hair as I spread
the dust to surround and I close the coffin with one
final fistful of dirt. I visit her every day. Sometimes
with a wilted petal or two, I pour my tears to
moisten her grave. As the snow no longer
litters the ground and the wind softens its
whip, I visit her with a concentrated ray to
focus on her. Spring leaps into form,
soil is rich for harvest. She emerges
from the depths of the earth to
stand in full form. Girl of buried
sins and flaws now woman
of repentance and faith.
May we all grow to
full bloom.

Gardener of Paradise

Baba plants 21 roses while
the sun slips its light to our work and retreats into the horizon,
and my Lord sends us a cool breeze as
we plant seeds of sweat and trickles of blood pricked by thorns.

As we toil and dig to place them within rain-softened soils,
we beg the Sustainer to allow our efforts to be fruitful.

Baba seeks the finest specimens of the most bountiful blooms to plant
vibrant colors; some are bushes some are climbers
others aren't included in the final plotting
because the hope of their survival is not enough, they must thrive.

They must thrive because these petals are not picked for this world,
they are meant to provide relief to the resting.
Baba wants enough roses to lay at every grave,
so the cemetery becomes a garden,
so the resting rest assured of the promised Gardens
with the coolness of countless petals bringing rehmat
while we stand making dhikr for the deceased.[2]

---

2   Sahih al-Bukhari 216: Narrated by Ibn Abbas, "Once the Prophet, while passing through one of the graveyards of Medina or Mecca heard the voices of two persons who were being tortured in their graves...The Prophet (ﷺ) then asked for a green leaf of a date-palm tree, broke it into two pieces and put one on each grave. On being asked why he had done so, he replied, "I hope that their torture might be lessened, till these get dried."

To plant a garden is to believe in tomorrow, and
Baba doesn't plant for his own enjoyment,
his iman flowers ours
as his calloused hands coax the buds to bloom,
and he builds for himself a home in Paradise
InshaAllah
by his niyyah for these roses that rest
at every grave.

Recipes of Success Here & After

Mumma was already a mother to three / when she learned how to cook / out of need to feed these little mouths / one day / she caught a glimmer of curiosity / and brought out the step stool / so I could watch her cook / now / I tower over and stir alongside / she teaches me /step by step / that measuring cups are useless / we must rely on the gifts of God / the taste / the smell / the visuals of our dishes / there is a correct browning of onions / and we should be able to identify / tangy tamarind in this mix / I carry spices in my skin / and recipes in my fingertips / passed down through my pulse / tracing my veins to my roots / and to mumma / while we cook / we speak in poems / about the mercy of our Rabb / mumma reminds me that we must carry ourselves / with the ability to answer to Allah / for every ounce / of every action / everything we want in life is better / bite-size / it always leaves us open to more / but still keeps us satisfied with what we've had / how everything assembles itself in our cuisine is a testament / to how melting pots are better as mosaics / we all deserve to shine / independently / while growing ourselves a better palate for / collaboration / and maybe world peace / pass the peas and add in a little more salt / the signs of goodness are everywhere / and we need to remember to recognize Who sent them / to pour into the dunya / what our Rabb asks of us / basks us in the marinade of deen / every essence flavored spiritually / mumma says when people engage with us / we should waft the sweetest iman / all we need is / a little bit more / of that one thing I can't translate to english / bear with me / the aroma of a life this savory / is worth it

The Gardens Beneath Which Rivers Flow

I am grown from the supplications of my elders and my ancestors
watered with hopes of Paradise and careful serums of the most fragrant deeds
each one woven into the essence of my soul
crafted to fit with the flowers that adorn the
Gardens beneath which rivers flow. I root seeds of
sadaqah in dunya and pray they bloom in eternal soils in the seven skies
yet I am trapped in the weeds of the world, unable to curate
arrangements from the streams of
strain and restlessness.
The blood in my veins is but water aching to meet streams of milk and honey,
with waves of pearls nestled in the riverbanks
my skin yearns to feel the breeze of the Heavens
in the courtyard of my Beloved as those he ﷺ loves
gather to hear the narrations of stories filled with trials and
triumphs
that build our love for him ﷺ and for Islam
every day my brown eyes dive deep in front of the mirror
meticulously in search of the perfect wudu that'll make my face glow on
that Day
my ears tense to catch the sound of the adhan
and any mention of my Beloved ﷺ
I pray my small moments are enough effort of servitude to my Lord
I was created to rest in the Gardens beneath which rivers flow but
I worry the heat in my heart will weigh heavy on that Day

I worry that I will be lost. I ask first my Lord to guide

        but on that day, I ask you my Beloved ﷺ to hold my hand

  I ask for a comfort no one else can give

      I ask for your intercession. Oh Beloved of my Lord ﷺ

          lead me to the Gardens beneath which rivers flow

Living up to Namesakes and Namegivers

We were hand-formed by baba's strength as much as we were by his love of storm chasers and Animal Planet, and we were stitched into our full potential as we sat at

mumma's feet, hopeful for a breeze of Paradise. *Dawn* breaks the horizon and we talk with her for hours about deen and dunya and everything in between. my siblings carry

Brilliance in every field imaginable because we were taught to adapt and to explore. so-called general knowledge ingrained into each fiber of our being *Uniquely* allowed us to

begin with a nuqta and change the trajectory of a generation. fisabillilah, we wage war *Bravely*, battling each other and still bunkering within ourselves; fortified against the

whole world as one. we were raised as *Truth-seekers*, to know our truth and walk in it. to follow Haqq and call to it. now as we grow in age and in distance, I pray we *Nurture*

ourselves, each other, and those around us, bearing the fruits of our namesakes and our name-givers. may we be worthy of them as their humble companions in Jannah.

Ameen.

Author Notes

The poem *"Our Ancestors Did Not Breathe This Air:* but I do, and so do you" on page 27 was written after the anthology *Our Ancestors Did Not Breathe This Air* by Afeefah Khazi-Syed, Aleena Shabbir, Ayse Angela Guvenilir, Maisha Munawwara Prome, Mariam Eman Dogar, and Marwa Abdullhai.

The poem "All the words I love are poems" on page 29 was written after Michelle Peñaloza's "All the Words I Can Remember Are Poems"

The poem "Living up to Namesakes and Namegivers" on page 60 italicizes the meanings of my siblings' and my names in birth order: Saher, Saniya, Shazia, Shujauddin, Salman, and Samreen. Only the major defining aspects are italicized but each name has weight, history, intention, and power. May we all live up to them and fulfill them justly, ameen.

Acknowledgements

All praise to Allah, the Most Merciful, the Most Compassionate. Anything good found in me and my work belongs first and foremost to Him, and then to my parents. I am endlessly grateful for the blessings and support I have received throughout this journey, and I am honored to have gotten to this point. My poetry has always been an act of ibadah so while I hope audiences enjoy it, I pray that it is accepted as well.

My parents are my inspiration and my world. Baba, you are easy to write about – your actions are inherently poetic. Your inspiring vision for the Ummah makes your lens a privilege to convey. Your heart is gold and its value anmol, and I am honored to carry your story and soul onward. Mumma, you are not so easy to write about – we speak in poetry. Our conversations are poetic, our mundane is poetic. To write about you is to capture poetry in motion and ask it to sit quietly, contained on a page. Your heart is gold and the weight is heavy, I am honored to carry your story and soul onward. I hope I carry both of your legacies in my veins, in my mannerisms, and in my worldview. I pray I've done you both some justice.

Amal Kassir, Sara Bawany, and Salma and the House of Amal family; thank you for being my mentors, my colleagues, and my sounding boards. You've pushed my creative bounds, nurtured my creative identity, and helped me hone my craft. I am forever grateful.

This book was written through the inaugural 2023 House of Amal writing cohort program.

Lastly, but certainly not least: thank you to the Strange Inc. publishing team for investing in me and this collection. May Allah SWT grant you all endless success in your endeavors and reward you for your efforts, ameen.

About The Author

Saniya Ruqiah Ahmed began her journey as a spoken word and slam poet in the realm of social justice advocacy. For nearly a decade, her art has been kept within the ears of her audience, and she is now aiming to bring her work to paper. Her poetry centers on themes like family, faith, social justice, and Muslim and Indian diaspora. Now as a medical student in the midwest, her poetry also encompasses humanity and dignity in healthcare. Her debut collection Hum Dum aims to be a companion to readers as an authentic, unapologetic, and powerful voice.

About Strange Inc.

Strange Inc. is dedicated to empowering Muslim women's voices worldwide. With a faith-based approach and a commitment to truthfulness and excellence, they unite creatives, using art to heal and reclaim identities. Through publications, writing shows, and support groups, they strive to amplify authentic voices and dispel misrepresentations. Their unwavering mission is to promote religious freedom, integrity, and cultural expression. Learn more at www.strangeincorporated.org

www.ingramcontent.com/pod-product-compliance
Lightning Source LLC
Chambersburg PA
CBHW010940120626
46554CB00008B/2545